Perspectives
Sharing the River
What Are the Issues?

Flying Start
to Literacy®

Contents

Introduction

How can we protect our rivers when they are used by so many?

Rivers are our lifeline. They provide us with drinking water and water for our crops, while also providing a home for wildlife. They are places where we can fish, swim, go boating and enjoy nature. And for some people, rivers are sacred. We must protect them!

But how can this be done? How can we use our rivers in different ways and for different purposes? How can we keep them clean and healthy?

Who uses the rivers?

Here are some facts about rivers that highlight their importance to us. Which fact surprises you the most? Why?

Rivers around the world

Around the world, 91 per cent of countries have at least one river. Most have many more. Australia has over 400 rivers, and New Zealand has 70 major river systems.

Cities

Most of the world's largest cities are built on rivers. In Australia, six of the eight capital cities are built on a river.

Water

Rivers drain nearly 75 per cent of the earth's land surface. In other words, when rain falls, three-quarters of it flows over land and into rivers.

Habitats

Rivers provide wildlife with food and a place to live. There are more than 10,000 species of known freshwater fish in the world.

Energy

The flow of water in rivers can be used to generate electricity. This hydroelectricity provides 16 per cent of the world's power.

River systems

Farming

Almost 70 per cent of fresh water in the world is used for farming. It is used to water crops and as drinking water for livestock such as cows.

It's my river!

Many people live along a river. But what happens when a river runs through a person's property? asks Joshua Hatch. Who is responsible for the river?

Property owner

I bought my farm because of this river. The property was in bad shape back then, but I spent tens of thousands of dollars to clean it up. I knew it could be beautiful again. I planted new trees along the banks and pulled debris from the water. I restocked fish and helped make the river healthy again.

Now, I like to sit on my verandah and watch the sun set over the water. The only problem is that other people like to fish on this river and they can only get to it through my property. I don't mind sharing my peaceful river, but I get angry when people blast loud music or leave plastic bottles and other rubbish behind.

Why should I have to put up with that? They're ruining my oasis. I paid for this, not them. I cleaned it up, not them. If they want to use my property to get to the river, that's fine. But I shouldn't have to clean up after them.

Environmentalist

When I was a little girl, my dad and I would walk along the river and look at the sparkly rainbow trout swimming in the clear water. Now, I'm a mother myself and recently, I took my kids to the same river I walked with my dad. The river runs through land owned by a mining company. I wanted to show my son and daughter the colourful trout, but the fish were gone. And the water wasn't clear anymore. It was opaque and brown.

This is because the mining company lets pollutants run off into the waterway. And the pollution doesn't stop at the property line. It flows down the stream and into the larger river basin.

The river basin is where we get our drinking water. It's where farmers draw water to put on their crops. Letting a private company pollute our water isn't just bad for the fish, it's bad for all of us.

Camper

My friends and I have been camping on the banks of this river for years. It's right next to a farm.

We like to get up early and paddle down the river. Herons watch us from the shore. Turtles slide off their logs as we pass by. Floating on the water as the sun rises overhead is an idyllic way to get away from the madness of the city. And I always look forward to our camping and canoeing holiday.

But today when we arrived at the campsite, there were signs that read Private Property, No Trespassing and Keep Out! We couldn't believe it. A person from the farm told us we couldn't camp here.

Why would they do this? They don't own the river, so we should be allowed to camp on the banks of the river.

To dam or not to dam?

Dams are incredible feats of engineering that allow us to store and share precious water.

But some people see dams differently. In this article, Kerrie Shanahan explains how these huge structures have devastated natural ecosystems and caused long-term environmental problems.

But the question is: How can we share our rivers fairly?

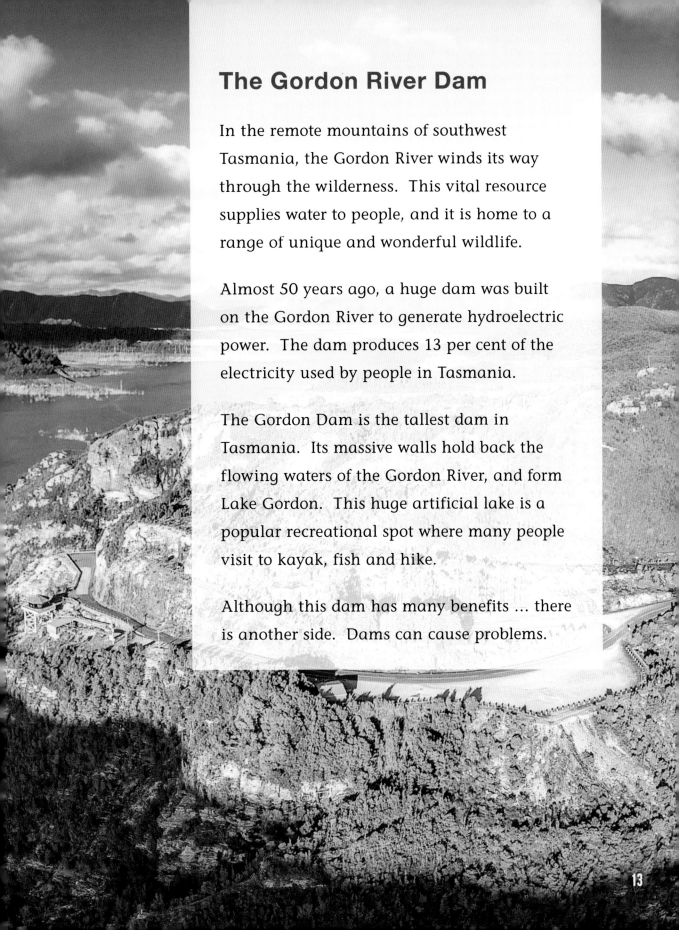

The Gordon River Dam

In the remote mountains of southwest Tasmania, the Gordon River winds its way through the wilderness. This vital resource supplies water to people, and it is home to a range of unique and wonderful wildlife.

Almost 50 years ago, a huge dam was built on the Gordon River to generate hydroelectric power. The dam produces 13 per cent of the electricity used by people in Tasmania.

The Gordon Dam is the tallest dam in Tasmania. Its massive walls hold back the flowing waters of the Gordon River, and form Lake Gordon. This huge artificial lake is a popular recreational spot where many people visit to kayak, fish and hike.

Although this dam has many benefits ... there is another side. Dams can cause problems.

Environmental problems

When a river is dammed, there can be major changes to many habitats. When the Gordon River was dammed to form Lake Gordon, whole habitats were flooded, killing animals and plants. Water also flooded close by Lake Pedder, destroying even more natural habitat.

The temperature of the water changes when dams are built, and some fish cannot live in the warmer or cooler waters. This can cause fish species to become extinct. When Lake Pedder was flooded, Australia's most endangered fish species, the Pedder galaxias, became extinct.

Dams change a river's flow

The flow of a river changes when a dam is built. Dams provide water for one area, but places further down the river have less water.

When the Gordon Dam was completed, there were plans to build a new dam downstream, where the Gordon River runs into the Franklin River.

▲ The Franklin River in southwestern Tasmania is one of the few wild rivers remaining in Australia.

◄ The Australian grayling (*Prototroctes maraena*) lives in the lower reaches of the Gordon River and is listed as "vulnerable" on the *Tasmanian Threatened Species Protection Act 1995*. Their preferred habitat is deep, slow flowing pools.

Many people protested against building the Franklin Dam. They were concerned that it would restrict the flow of water. They were also concerned that large areas of habitat would be flooded, damaging the wildlife around the rivers. Eventually, the plan was abolished and the Franklin Dam was never built.

We all rely on fresh water and power. What is the balance between protecting our environment and accessing life-giving river water? Who should decide?

The river protectors

What would happen if we changed how we treated objects in nature and began to see them as living things, equal to human beings and with the same legal rights? asks environmental lawyer John Gillespie. How would it change how you think about places in nature such as rivers and forests?

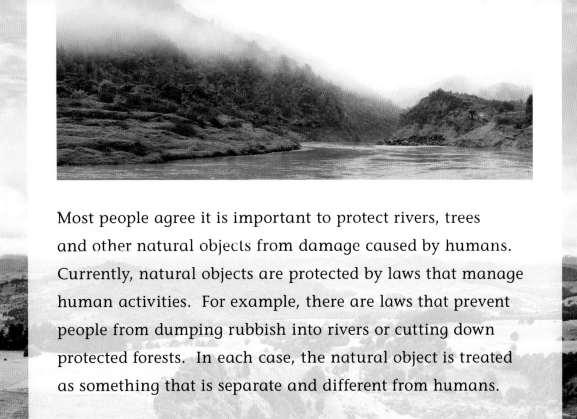

Most people agree it is important to protect rivers, trees and other natural objects from damage caused by humans. Currently, natural objects are protected by laws that manage human activities. For example, there are laws that prevent people from dumping rubbish into rivers or cutting down protected forests. In each case, the natural object is treated as something that is separate and different from humans.

But First Peoples in many countries treat nature differently. In 2017, the New Zealand Parliament passed the *Te Awa Tupua (Whanganui River Claims Settlement) Act 2017*, a law which granted the Whanganui River the same legal rights as a person. The decision ended a long court case between the New Zealand Government and the Māori. This was the first time such a law had ever been passed.

For many years, the Government had used the Whanganui River for transport and mining for minerals. This caused pollution, destroyed fisheries and degraded the river's cultural and spiritual value.

The Act recognised that the Māori not only rely on the river for food and water but also take their name, spirit and strength from the river . In Māori culture, *tupuna*, or "ancestors", are a part of nature and are especially in and around rivers. This close relationship is shown in the traditional saying "I am the river, the river is me".

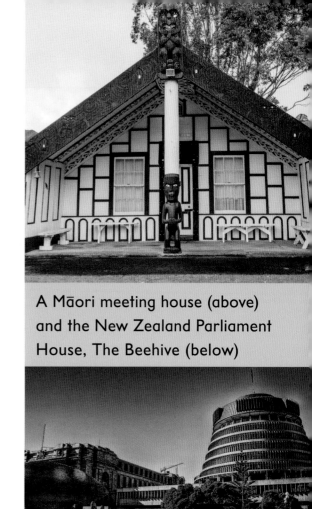

A Māori meeting house (above) and the New Zealand Parliament House, The Beehive (below)

This is the first time in the world that a river has been given legal rights.
This means that law courts can recognise the right of the Whanganui
River to take legal action against people who cause it harm.

Of course, it is not the river that takes the legal action. Two people –
one from the Māori and another from the government – will be in
charge of acting on the river's behalf to protect it.

What killed the Fish?

In 2019, fishermen visiting the Menindee Lakes in western New South Wales were shocked to see thousands of dead fish floating in the lake. The water flowing through this part of the Murray–Darling Basin was too low for the fish to survive.

Over 15 years ago, the Federal Government made a law called the *Water Act 2007*. Its purpose was to protect the Murray–Darling Basin. But is it enough? How can we stop the fish from dying?

Fish deaths during periods of drought and low water flows are normal. What was unprecedented at the Menindee Lakes in 2019 was the number of fish deaths. Scientists estimate that over a million fish died during three mass fish death events.

They are in no doubt about what caused the deaths. The fish died because the water flows were too low, which allowed algae to bloom and reduce the oxygen dissolved in the water. Fish breathe dissolved oxygen through their gills.

Although water flows increase and decrease during wet and dry years, too much water had been taken out of the Darling River. This is the river that feeds water into the Menindee Lakes.

The Darling River is part of the Murray–Darling river system, which irrigates Australia's largest food-growing area. For many years, farmers along the Darling River have been using water from the river in ever-increasing volumes for water-hungry crops like cotton. It is estimated that water flows into the lakes have been reduced by half over the last 20 to 30 years.

In 2007, the Australian Federal Government introduced the *Water Act 2007*. The purpose of this law was to set up the Murray–Darling Basin Authority. It is the responsibility of the Murray–Darling Basin Authority to balance the farmers' need for water with the need to provide enough water to protect the environment. This is called the environmental flow.

Since the Act was introduced, the Federal Government has increased the amount of water available to farmers, and this has reduced the environmental flow. Adding to the environmental problems, scientists say that the Murray–Darling Basin Authority has not protected the river during periods of drought by failing to ensure there was enough environmental flow to protect the fish.

If they increased the environmental flow in times of drought, the Authority could flush the river system to reduce the growth of algae and ensure there is enough oxygen for the fish to live.

What is your opinion? How to write a persuasive argument

1. State your opinion

Think about the issues related to your topic. What is your opinion?

2. Research

Research the information you need to support your opinion.

Related *Perspectives* book   Internet   Other sources

3. Make a plan

Introduction

How will you "hook" the reader?

State your opinion.

List reasons to support your opinion.

What persuasive devices will you use?

Reason 1
Support your reason with evidence and details.

Reason 2
Support your reason with evidence and details.

Reason 3
Support your reason with evidence and details.

Conclusion

Restate your opinion. Leave your reader with a strong message.

4. Publish

Publish your persuasive argument.

Use visuals to reinforce your opinion.